I Can Do It!
Piano Book

First Book of Favorite Songs

by Christine Bemko Kril
Illustrated by Patricia Carmody

KĀPOK PRESS
Fredericksburg, Virginia

P.O. Box 1861
Fredericksburg, VA 22402-1861
866-44-KĀPOK (52765)
email: kapokpress@msn.com

To order products visit us online at www.kapokpress.com

*I would like to thank my family, friends, students and colleagues
who encouraged me in the creation of this book. My special thanks go to
Natalie Bemko-Burno and the young students at Carey School who
were my earliest supporters. This book is dedicated to the memory of
Ivan John Kril - wonderful husband and best friend.*
Christine Bemko Kril

Published in Fredericksburg, Virginia

Library of Congress Control Number: 2004093179

ISBN 0-9718477-0-3

Printed in China

Introduction

Dear Parents and Friends,

This book is for children and adults who wish to play the piano or keyboard and need a place to start. Here beginners can learn the names of the keys, learn to use all of their fingers to play, explore the instrument, play favorite songs, and have fun making music.

Your child may need your help to remove the charts from the front cover. Follow the directions in **Get Ready**, **Get Set**, **Go!** and you are on your way. In the beginning it's easier to learn to play if you follow the pages in order. Keep the fingering chart on the music holder of your piano, next to the book, to help you know which finger to use on which key. Read the **Play** pages and **Exploration Fun** page to learn more about music and playing the piano.

This book is intended as a first step in the discovery of music and music making. If you love what you learn here and do not yet have a teacher, plcasc consider piano lessons with a qualified, caring professional. Music can become a most valuable part of your children's lives, and the lives of those around them.

Let's encourage the next generation of musicians.

Christine Bemko Kril

Table of Contents

Fingering and Keyboard Chart - see front cover
(also printed on pg. 80 - copying permitted only for use with this book)

Get Ready!

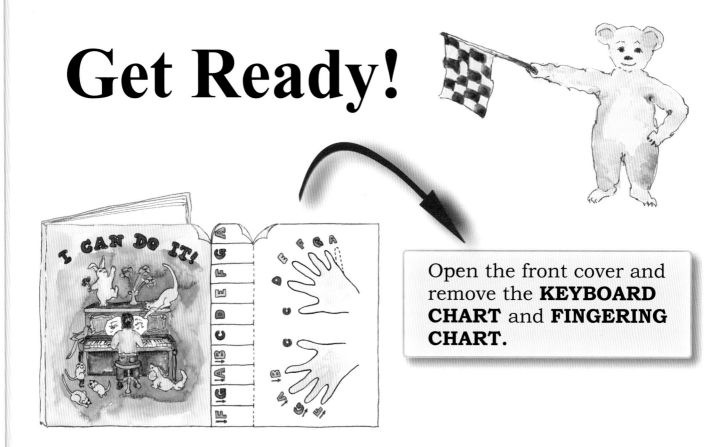

Open the front cover and remove the **KEYBOARD CHART** and **FINGERING CHART**.

KEYBOARD CHART
These are the names of the keys on the piano.

FINGERING CHART
Keep this chart handy to use when you get to the **Finger Play** pages.

Remember:
your **left hand** plays letters with ⬇ **Arrows**.

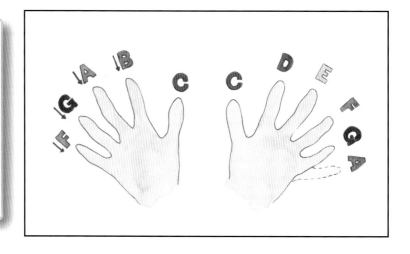

Get Set...

Stand the **KEYBOARD CHART** behind the keys.

Find the **DOG** on your chart and let's put him in a **DOGHOUSE**.

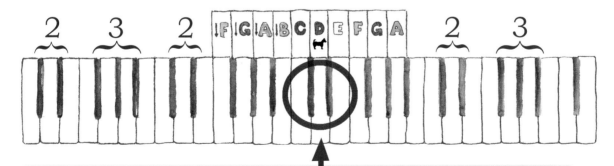

Look for groups of **two** and **three** black keys on your keyboard.

A **DOGHOUSE** is a *group of two* black keys.

Go!

To Play:

First press

Then press

Then press

You did it!

Remember: relax and take your time. Sit a little away from the keyboard, so you have room to move your arms.

Hot Cross Buns

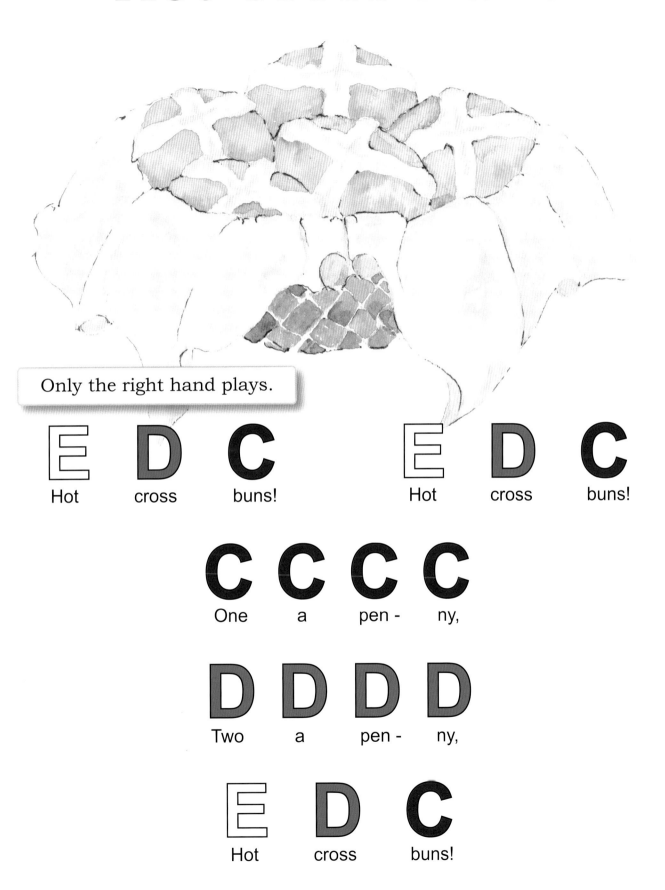

Only the right hand plays.

E	D	C		E	D	C
Hot	cross	buns!		Hot	cross	buns!

C	C	C	C
One	a	pen -	ny,

D	D	D	D
Two	a	pen -	ny,

E	D	C
Hot	cross	buns!

Up We Go!

Allegro (ah-leh-groh) - this Italian word
tells you that this song is *fast and cheerful*.

Only the right hand plays.

C	D	C	D	E
Up	and	down	we	go!

E	C	E	D	C
Skip	down,	then	a	row.

Easter Bunny

Giocoso (joh-koh-soh) - this Italian word
tells you that this song is *merry and happy.*

Only the right hand plays.

C   **D**   E   F   **G**

Bun - ny   goes   to   G,

G   F   E   **D**   C

Now   he's   back   to   C.

Finger Play • Right Hand

Put your **right hand** on the **FINGERING CHART**.
Look to see which **letter** matches each finger.
Look to see which **number** matches each finger.

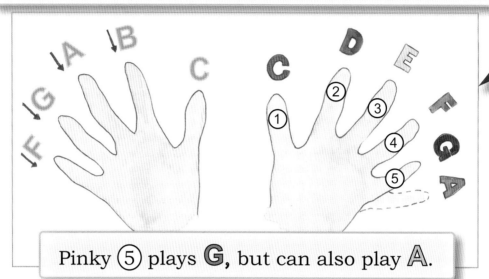

Pinky ⑤ plays **G,** but can also play **A**.

Put your **right hand** on the keyboard and match each finger
to its own key.

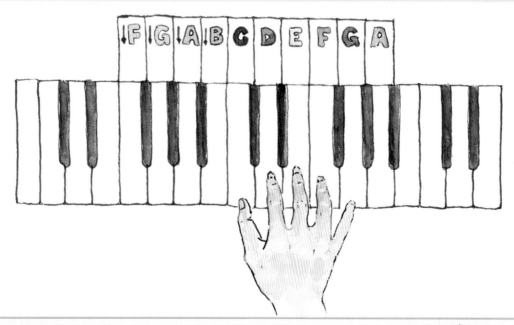

Now play the warm up on the next page. ➡

Warm Up!

Use all the fingers of your **right hand** to play this warm up.
Start with **thumb** ① on **C** and go up to **pinky** ⑤ on **G**.

C   D   E   F   G

Now start with **pinky** ⑤ on **G** and go down to **thumb** ① on **C**.

G   F   E   D   C

Play two times largo
(lahr-goh) - *slowly*.

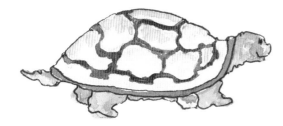

Play two times vivace
(vee-vah-chay) - *quickly*.

You did it! Play this warm up every day.

Play the next song with all the fingers of your right hand.

Mary Had a Little Lamb

Dolce (dol-chay) - play *gently and sweetly.*

Words by Sarah
Josepha Hale, 1830

E D C D

Mar - y   had   a

E E E

lit -   tle   lamb,

D D D

Lit -   tle   lamb,

E G G

lit -   tle   lamb,

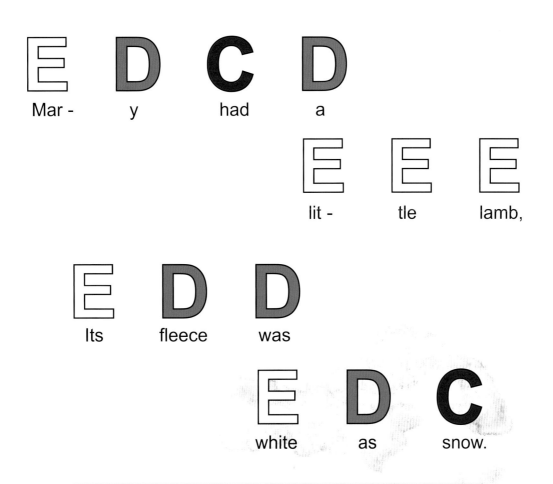

E D C D
Mar - y had a

E E E
lit - tle lamb,

E D D
Its fleece was

E D C
white as snow.

Verses: *play this song again* with new words.

Everywhere that Mary went,
Mary went, Mary went,
Everywhere that Mary went
the lamb was sure to go.

It followed her to school one day,
School one day, school one day,
It followed her to school one day,
That was against the rule.

It made the children laugh and play,
Laugh and play, laugh and play,
It made the children laugh and play
to see a lamb at school.

When the Saints Go Marching In

March - music for a *parade*.

Traditional

C E **F** G
Oh, when the Saints —

C E **F** G
go march - ing in, —

C E **F** G
Oh, when the Saints

E **C** E **D**
go march - ing in, —

16

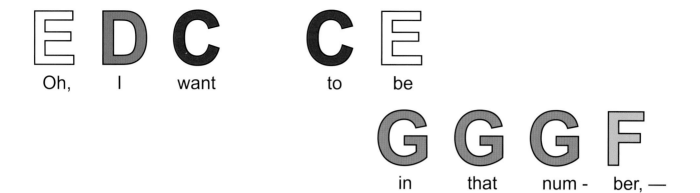

E D C   C E
Oh,   I   want   to   be

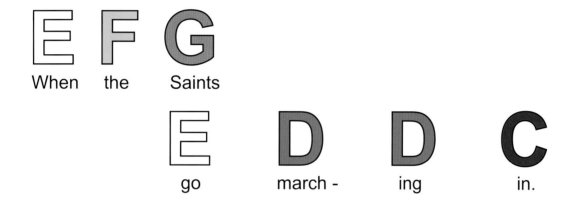

G G G F
in   that   num -   ber, —

E F G
When   the   Saints

E D D C
go   march -   ing   in.

Second verse:

Oh, when those bells begin to ring,
Oh, when those bells begin to ring,
Oh, I want to be in that number,
When those bells begin to ring.

Twinkle, Twinkle, Little Star

Put your **right hand thumb** on **D** to play this song. ④ means play **G** with your **ring finger**. ⑤ means play **A** with your **pinky**.

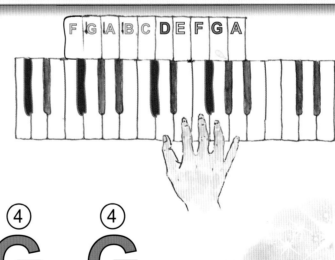

Play **C** with your **left** hand thumb.

C	C	④ G	④ G
Twin -	kle,	twin -	kle,

⑤ A	⑤ A	④ G
lit -	tle	star,

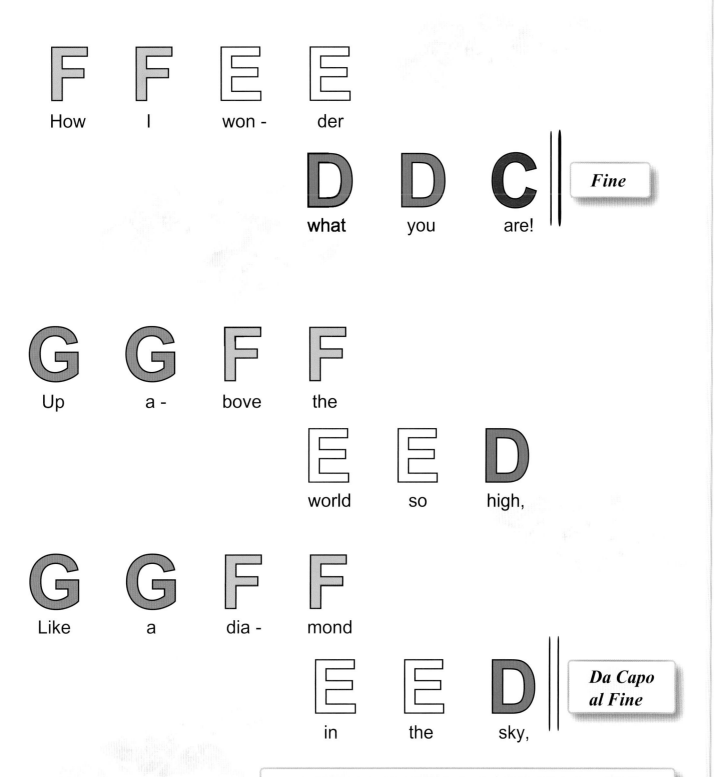

F F E E
How I won - der

D D C
what you are! *Fine*

G G F F
Up a - bove the

E E D
world so high,

G G F F
Like a dia - mond

E E D
in the sky, *Da Capo al Fine*

Da Capo al Fine (dah kah-poh ahl fee-nay) - play again from the beginning, and stop at *Fine* (fee-nay) which means *The End*.

19

Low and High

Some sounds are **high**.

Some sounds are **low**.

Play some keys on your keyboard, one right after the other. Do the sounds get *lower* or *higher*? Sing the sounds you play to help you decide.

LOWER ←   **HIGHER** →

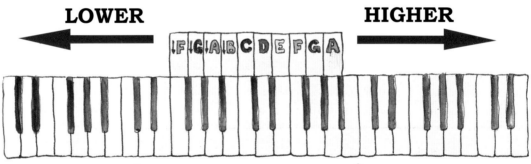

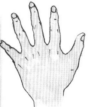

Play some **low** keys with your **left** hand.

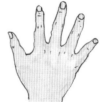

Play some **high** keys with your **right** hand.

Play letters with ↓ arrows with your **LEFT HAND**. These are **lower** keys.

Wake Up Song

(Reveille)

Play ↓**G** with your *left hand.*

Morning Bugle Call

It's   time

to   get   up,

It's   time

to   get   up,

It's   time

to   get   up

in   the   morn —   ing!

‖:   :‖ - *repeat signs* - play the part between these signs once more.

21

Ring Around the Rosie

Play ↓B and ↓G with your *left hand.*
Play the other letters with your *right hand.*

Singing Game

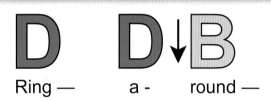

D   D↓B

Ring —   a -   round —

ED   ↓B

the   ros ——   ie,

↓B D   D↓B

A   pock —   et   full —

ED   ↓B

of   po ——   sies,

D **↓B**
Ash — es!

D **↓B**
Ash — es!

C D **D ↓G**
We all — fall — down!

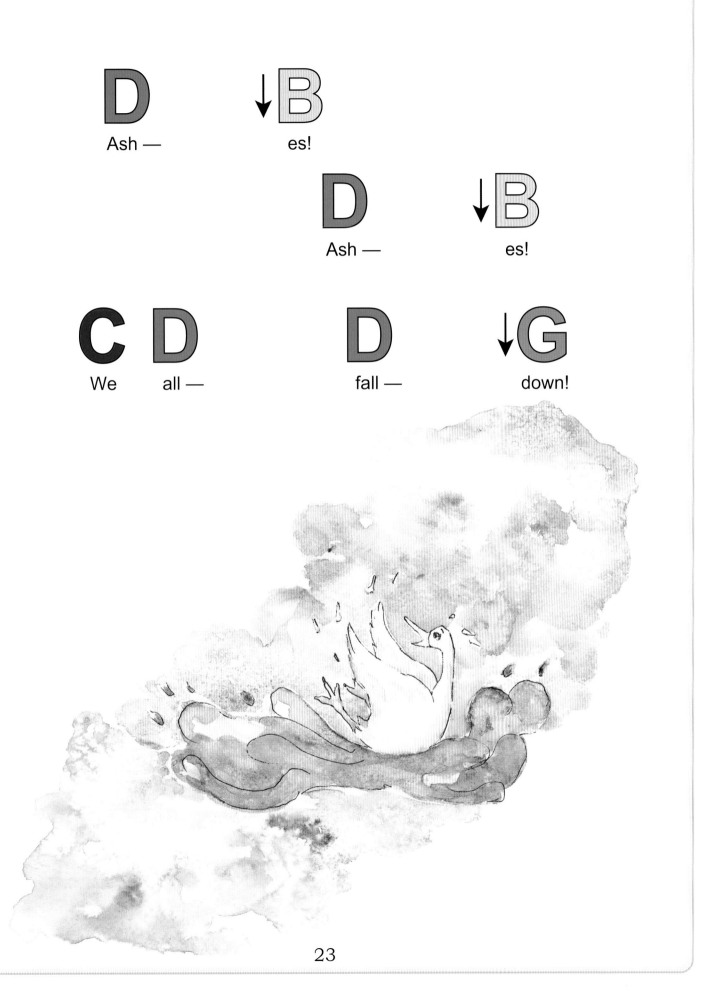

23

Finger Play • Left Hand

Put your **left hand** on the **FINGERING CHART**.
Look to see which **letter** matches each finger.
Look to see which **number** matches each finger.

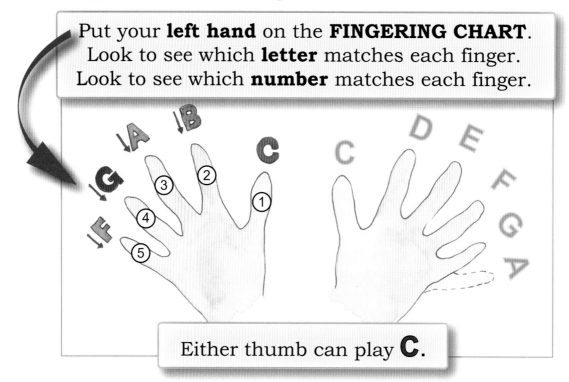

Either thumb can play **C**.

Put your **left hand** on the keyboard and match each finger
to its own key.

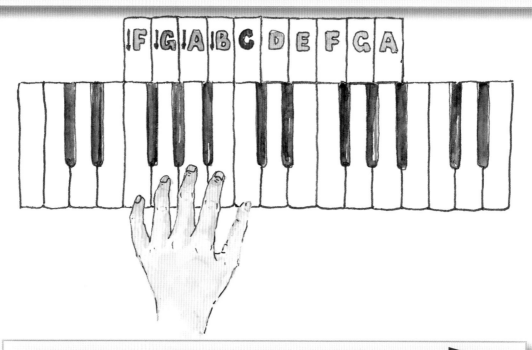

Play the warm up on the next page.

Warm Up!

Use all the fingers of your **left hand** to play this warm up.
Start with **thumb** ① on **C** and go to **pinky** ⑤ on **F**.

C B A G F

Now start with **pinky** ⑤ on **F** and go up to **thumb** ① on **C**.

F G A B C

Play two times largo
(lahr-goh) - *slowly*.

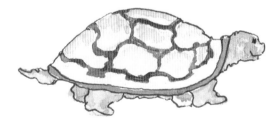

Play two times vivace
(vee-vah-chay) - *quickly*.

Good job! Play this warm up every day.

Use all the fingers of your left hand to play the next song.

Row Your Boat

Giocoso (joh-koh-soh) - *merry, happy.*

Traditional Round

⬇ Use your **left hand** to play letters with **arrows.**

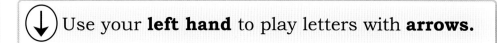

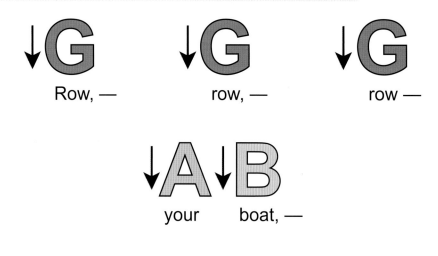

⬇**G** ⬇**G** ⬇**G**
Row, —   row, —   row —

⬇**A**⬇**B**
your   boat, —

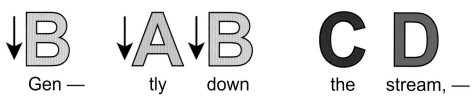

⬇**B**   ⬇**A**⬇**B**   **C D**
Gen —   tly down   the   stream, —

Mer - ri - ly,

mer - ri - ly,

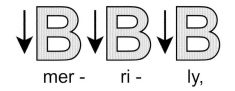

mer - ri - ly,

mer - ri - ly,

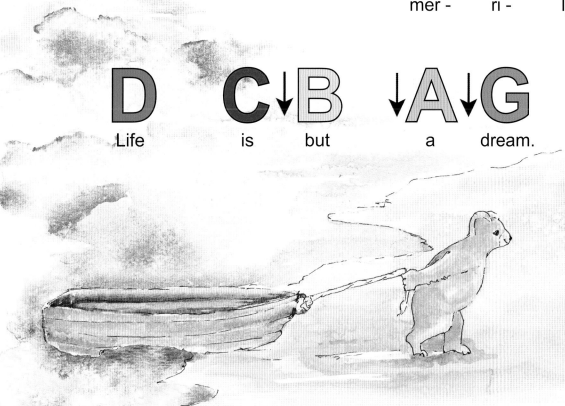

Life is but a dream.

Shortnin' Bread

Allegro (ah-leh-groh) - this song is *lively and fast.*

Play ↓G with your **left** hand. Play G with your **right** hand.

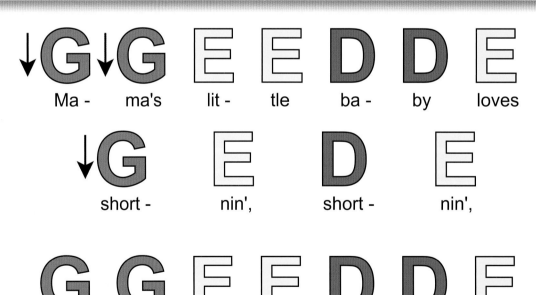

↓**G** ↓**G** E E **D** D E
Ma - ma's lit - tle ba - by loves

↓**G** E **D** E
short - nin', short - nin',

G **G** E E **D** D E
Ma - ma's lit - tle ba - by loves

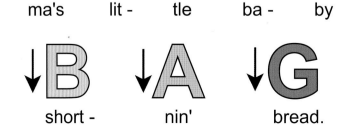

↓**B** ↓**A** ↓**G**
short - nin' bread.

Patterns!

The **first** and **third** lines of Shortnin' Bread
use the same letters:

↓G↓G E E D D E
G G E E D D E

This is called a **pattern**.
Something is different in the first line. What?

Now look at the **second** line of Shortnin' Bread.

↓G E D E

The letter pattern is the same,
but there is only one of each letter.

Every song has its own special patterns.
Here are some patterns to look for -

C D E or **E D C**

E F G or **G F E**

Find the letter pattern of a song you like and write it down.
Look for letter patterns in every song you play.

Find the patterns* in the next song - Yankee Doodle.
(*answers on pg. 31)

Yankee Doodle

| March - music for a *parade*. | Humorous American Revolutionary Song |

C   C   D   E

Yan -   kee   doo -   dle

C   E   D

went   to   town

↓G   C   C   D   E

a   rid -   ing   on   a

C   ↓B

po —   ny,

↓**G** **C** **C** **D** E

He   stuck   a   feath -   er

F E **D** **C**

in   his   cap   and

↓**B** ↓**G** ↓**A** ↓**B**

called   it   mac -   a -

C   **C**

ro —   ni!

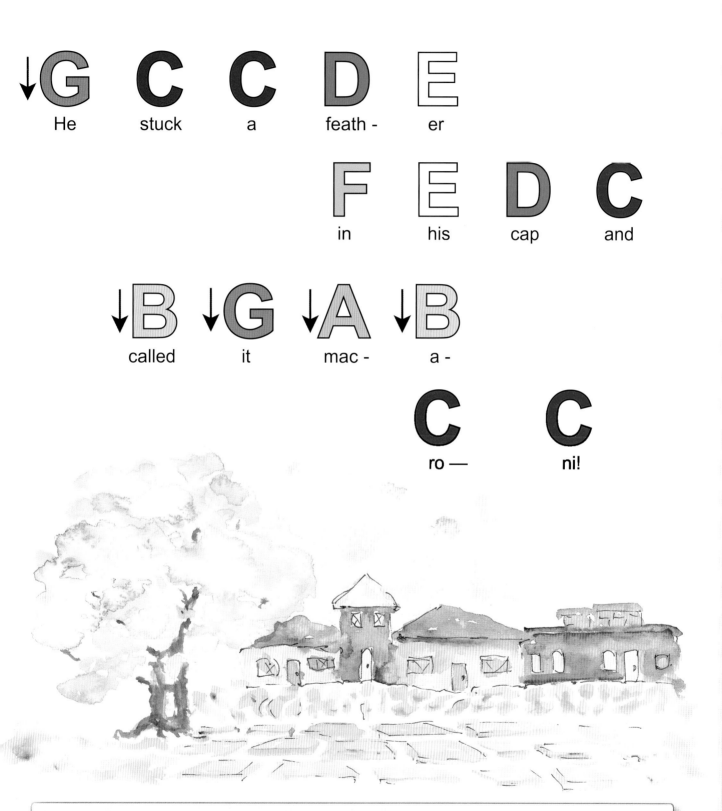

*Yankee Doodle has short and long patterns. Some short patterns are
C C, E **D** and **C**↓**B**. Some longer patterns are **C C D** E and ↓**G C C D** E.

31

Hickory, Dickory, Dock

From Tommy Thumb's
Pretty Song Book, c.1744

Allegretto (ah-leh-gret-oh) -
this song is *lively and quick,
but a bit slower than allegro.*

D E D

Hick - o - ry,

C ↓B C D (**G D**)
(Tick, tock!)

dick - o - ry, dock,

D D D C

The mouse ran up

↓A ↓B (**G D**)
(Tick, tock!)

the clock.

↓B ↓B ↓B D
the clock   struck one,

D C   C E
the mouse   ran down,

D E D
Hick -   o -   ry,

C ↓B ↓A ↓G (D G)
                    (Tick, tock!)
dick -   o -   ry,   dock.

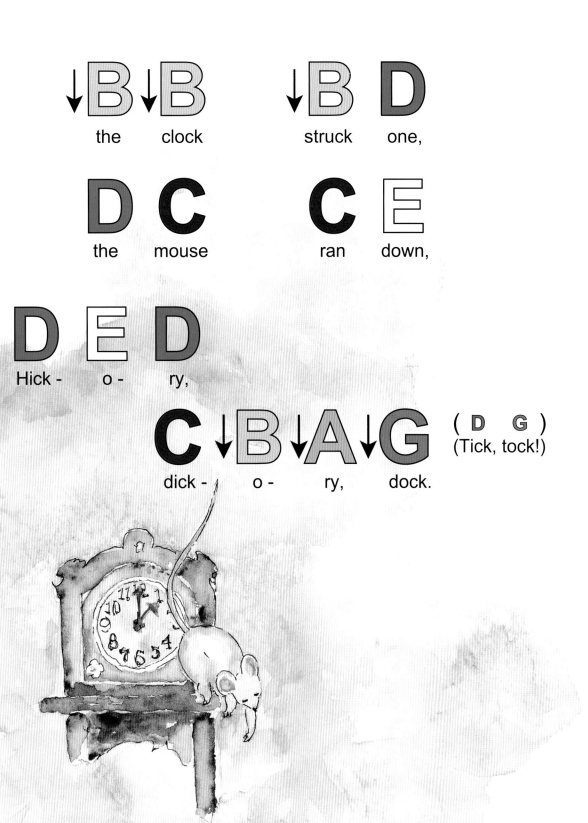

33

Fast and Slow

A lively song or dance
tune is **fast** - *allegro* (ah-leh-groh).

A lullaby that you sing
to put a baby to sleep is **slow** - *largo* (lahr-goh).

PARTS OF A SONG CAN BE SLOW OR FAST.

allegro - **FAST**   **CD**

largo - **SLOW**   **C**   **D**

vivace (vee-vah-chay)
- **VERY FAST**   **C͡D**

Play the letters under the curved lines
vivace - *very fast* - in *The Farmer in the Dell*.

Farmer in the Dell

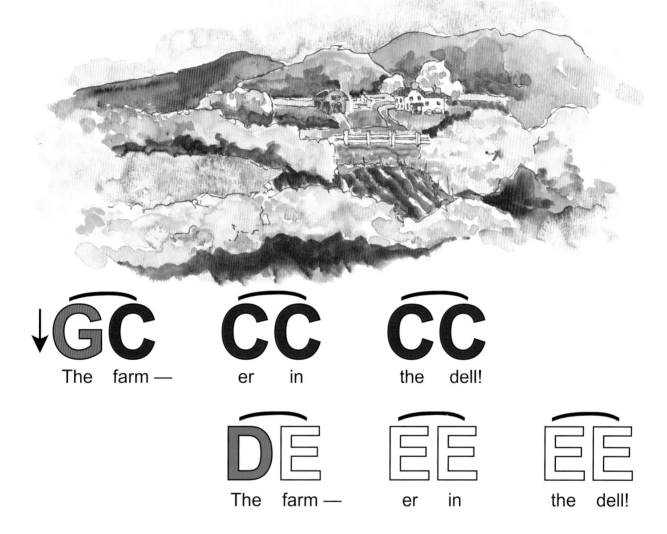

↓ G͡C   C͡C   C͡C
The farm — er in the dell!

D͡E   E͡E   E͡E
The farm — er in the dell!

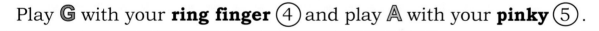

Play **G** with your **ring finger** ④ and play **A** with your **pinky** ⑤.

④   ④   ⑤ ④
G   G   A͡G   E͡C
Hi,   ho,   the mer —   ry o,

D͡E   E͡D   D͡C
The farm — er in the dell!

Shoo Fly

Spiritoso (spiri-toh-soh) - *with spirit.*

E **C**
Shoo   fly,

D **E** **F͡D**
don't   both —   er me!

D↓B
Shoo   fly,

C **D** **E͡C**
don't   both —   er me!

E **C**
Shoo fly,

D **E** **F** **D**
don't both — er me!

D **G** **G** **G**
For I be - long

F **E** **D** **C**
to some - bod - y!

37

Hush, Little Baby

Soave (swa-vey) - play this song *gently and smoothly.*

Lullaby

↓**G** E E E **F**

Hush,   lit - tle ba —   by,

E **DDD**

don't   say a word,

↓**G**↓**GDDD**

Ma - ma's gon - na buy

DE**D** **C** **C**

you a mock —   ing   bird.

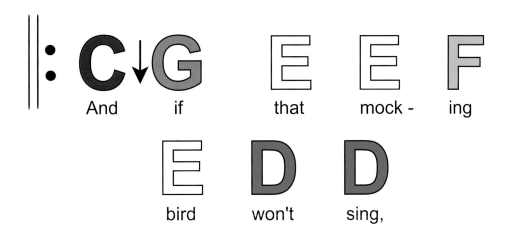

C G E E F
And if that mock- ing

E D D
bird won't sing,

G G D D D
Ma- ma's gon- na buy

D E D C C
you a dia- mond ring.

‖: :‖ - *repeat signs* - play the part between these signs again with new verses.

Verses:

And if that diamond ring turns brass,
Mama's gonna buy you a looking glass.

And if that looking glass gets broke,
Mama's gonna buy you a billy goat.

And if that billy goat don't pull,
Mama's gonna buy you a cart and bull.

And if that cart and bull turn over,
Mama's gonna buy you a dog named Rover.

Skip to My Lou

Allegretto (ah-leh-gret-oh) -
play this song *a little fast.*

Old Singing Game

E C

Lou,   Lou,

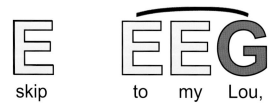

E   EEG

skip   to my Lou,

D ↓B

Lou,   Lou,

D   DDF

skip   to my Lou,

E C
Lou, Lou,

E EEG
skip to my Lou,

D EFE
Skip to my Lou

DC C
my dar — ling!

41

Here Comes the Bride

Grave (grah-veh) - play this music *slowly and solemnly.*

From R. Wagner's opera
Lohengrin, 1848

↓G   C   C͡C

↓G   D   ↓B͡C

↓G   C   F͡F   E   D͡C

D͡C↓B   C͡D

↓G C C͡C

↓G D ↓B͡C

↓G C E͡G E

C͡A↓ D E͡C

London Bridge

> Put your **right hand thumb** on **D** to play this song. ④ means play **G** with your **ring finger**. ⑤ means play **A** with your **pinky**.

Singing Game

④ ⑤ ④
G **A G** **F**
Lon -   don   Bridge   is

E **F** **G**
fall -   ing   down,

D **E** **F**
fall -   ing   down,

E **F** **G**
fall -   ing   down,

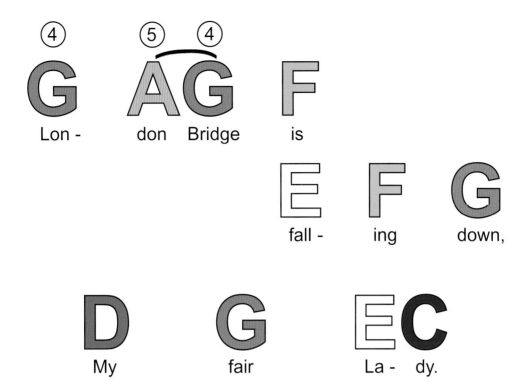

④ ⑤ ④
G A G F
Lon - don Bridge is

E F G
fall - ing down,

D G E C
My fair La - dy.

Verses:

Build it up with iron bars,
Iron bars, iron bars,
Build it up with iron bars,
My fair Lady.

Iron bars will bend and break,
Bend and break, bend and break,
Iron bars will bend and break,
My fair Lady.

Build it up with stones so strong,
Stones so strong, stones so strong,
Build it up with stones so strong,
My fair Lady.

Take a key and lock her up,
Lock her up, lock her up,
Take a key and lock her up,
My fair Lady.

Where is Thumbkin?

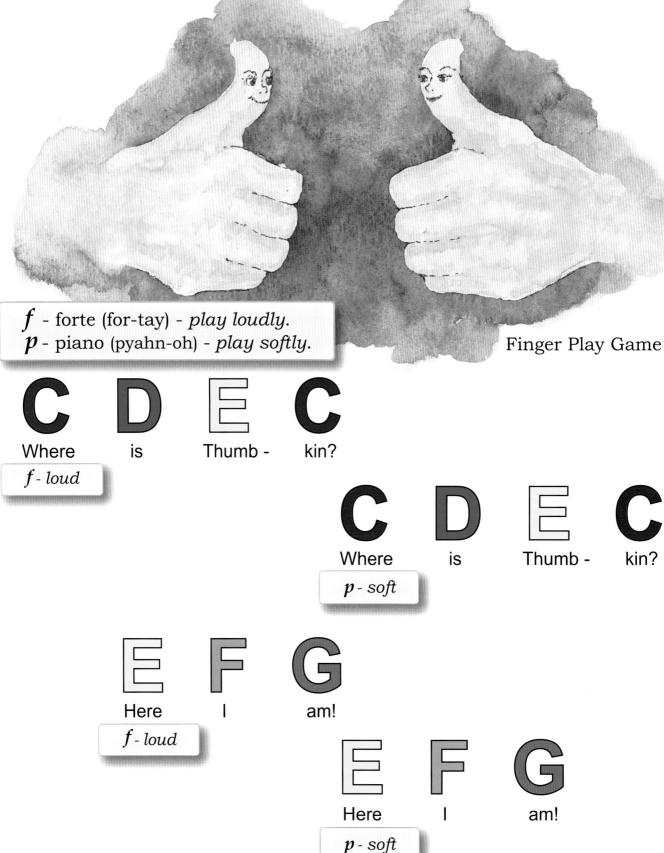

f - forte (for-tay) - *play loudly.*
p - piano (pyahn-oh) - *play softly.*

Finger Play Game

C **D** **E** **C**

Where   is   Thumb -   kin?

f - loud

C **D** **E** **C**

Where   is   Thumb -   kin?

p - soft

E **F** **G**

Here   I   am!

f - loud

E **F** **G**

Here   I   am!

p - soft

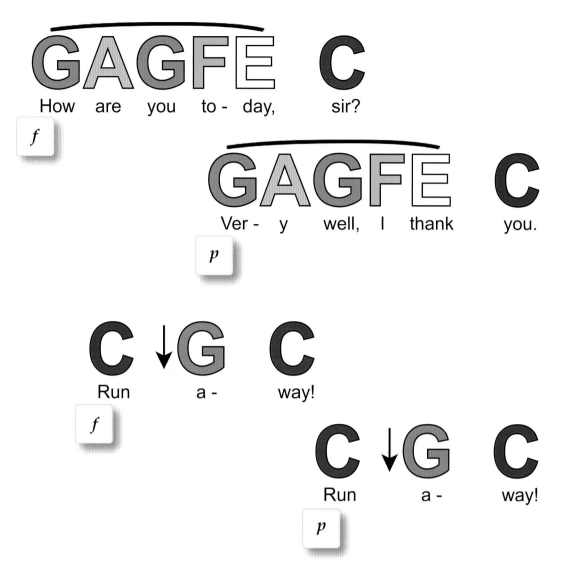

GAGFE C
How are you to - day, sir?

f

GAGFE C
Ver - y well, I thank you.

p

C ↓G C
Run a - way!

f

C ↓G C
Run a - way!

p

Verses *(only the first part changes)* :

2. Where is pointer? Where is pointer?
   Here I am, here......

3. Where is tall man? Where is tall man?
   Here I am, here......

4. Where is ring man? Where is ring man?
   Here I am, here......

5. Where is pinky? Where is pinky?
   Here I am, here......

This Old Man

Scherzando (sker-tsahn-doh) - *playfully.*

Old English
Folk Rhyme

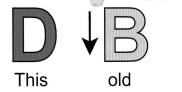

This   old   man,

he   played   one,

He   played   nick -   nack

on   my   thumb,

With a nick nack pad - dy whack,

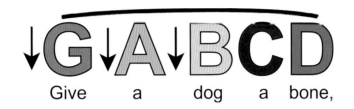

Give a dog a bone,

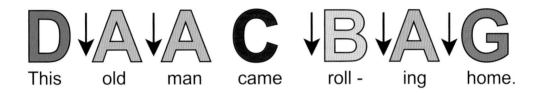

This old man came roll - ing home.

Verses:

2. This old man, he played **two**,
   He played nick-nack on my **shoe**...(Chorus: With a nick...)
3. This old man, he played **three**,
   He played nick-nack on my **knee**...(Chorus)
4. This old man, he played **four**,
   He played nick-nack on my **door**...(Chorus)
5. This old man, he played **five**,
   He played nick-nack on my **eye**...(Chorus)
6. This old man, he played **six**,
   He played nick-nack with **heel clicks**...(Chorus)
7. This old man, he played **seven**,
   He played nick-nack up in **heaven**...(Chorus)
8. This old man, he played **eight**,
   He played nick-nack on my **plate**...(Chorus)
9. This old man, he played **nine**,
   He played nick-nack on my **line**...(Chorus)
10. This old man, he played **ten**,
    He played nick-nack **once again**...(Chorus)

There's a Hole in the Bucket

Allegro (ah-leh-groh) - this song is *lively and quick.*

CDE   **C**

There's a   hole   in

↓**G**   ↓**A**   **C**

the   buck -   et,

↓**G**   ↓**A**   **C**

dear   Li -   za,

↓**G**   ↓**A**   **C**

dear   Li -   za,

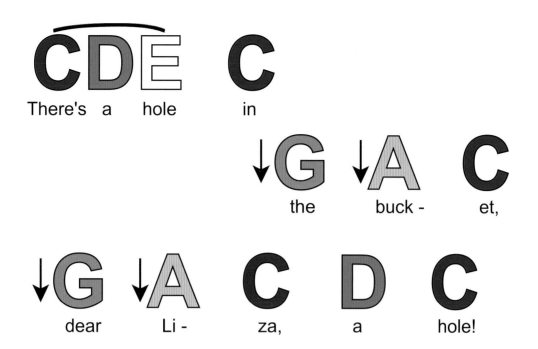

C D E C
There's a hole in

↓G ↓A C
the buck - et,

↓G ↓A C D C
dear Li - za, a hole!

Verses:

2. *Then mend it, dear Henry, dear Henry, dear Henry,*
   Then mend it, dear Henry, dear Henry, mend it!

   3. With what shall I mend it, dear Liza, dear Liza,
      With what shall I mend it, dear Liza, with what?

4. *With a straw, dear Henry, dear Henry, dear Henry,*
   With a straw, dear Henry, dear Henry, a straw!

   5. But the straw is too long, dear Liza, dear Liza,
      But the straw is too long, dear Liza, too long.

6. *Then cut it, dear Henry, dear Henry, dear Henry,*
   Then cut it, dear Henry, dear Henry, cut it!

   7. With what shall I cut it, dear Liza, dear Liza,
      With what shall I cut it, dear Liza, with what?

8. *With a knife, dear Henry, dear Henry, dear Henry,*
   With a knife, dear Henry, dear Henry, a knife!

   9. But the knife is too dull, dear Liza, dear Liza,
      But the knife is too dull, dear Liza, too dull.

10. *Then sharpen it, dear Henry, dear Henry, dear Henry,*
    Then sharpen it, dear Henry, dear Henry, sharpen it!

    11. But the stone is too dry, dear Liza, dear Liza,
        But the stone is too dry, dear Liza, too dry.

12. *Then wet it, dear Henry, dear Henry, dear Henry,*
    Then wet it, dear Henry, dear Henry, wet it!

    13. But there's a hole in the bucket, dear Liza, dear Liza,
        There's a hole in the bucket, dear Liza, a hole!

Michael, Row the Boat Ashore

Spiritoso (spiri-toh-soh) - *lively, with spirit.*

↓**G** ↓**B** **D**
Mi -   chael,   row

↓**B͡D** **E** **D**
the   boat   a -   shore,

↓**B** **D** **E** **D**
Al-   le -   lu ——————— ia!

Mi -   chael,   row

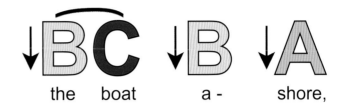

the   boat   a -   shore,

Al-   le -   lu ——

u ——————————   ia!

Verses:

Sister, help to trim the sail, Alleluia!
Sister, help to trim the sail, Alleluia!

River Jordan is wide and cold, Alleluia!
Chills the body but not the soul, Alleluia!

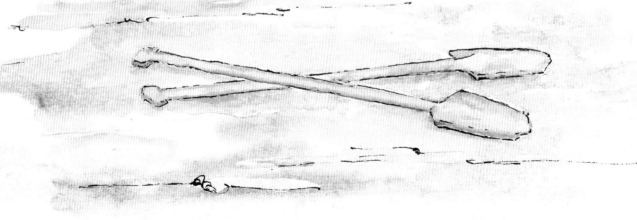

Old MacDonald

‖: • (↓**G**) **C C C ↓G**
  • 2. And   on   1. Old   Mac -   Don -   ald
                          his   farm -   he

> Play this first ↓**G** only on the second verse.

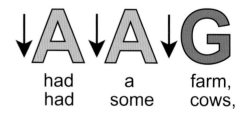

↓**A** ↓**A** ↓**G**
had   a   farm,
had   some   cows,

E E D D C :‖   *Fine*
e - i - e - i-   o!

> ‖: :‖ - *repeat signs*: play the part between these signs again with the second verse.

54

With   a   moo   moo   here,

And   a   moo   moo   there,

Here   a   moo,

there   a   moo,

Ev - 'ry   where   a   moo   moo!

Da Capo al Fine

Da Capo al Fine: go back and play the first verse again. Stop at the word ***Fine*** (fee-nay) which means *The End*.

Home On the Range

Giocoso (joh-koh-soh) - *merry, happy.*

Cowboy Song

↓**G** ↓**G** **C** **D** **E**

Oh,   give   me   a   home

C ↓**B̄A** **F** **F** **F**

where   the   buf -   fa -   lo   roam,

E **F̄G**

Where   the   deer

C **C̄C** ↓**B** **C** **D**

and   the   an -   te -   lope   play, ——

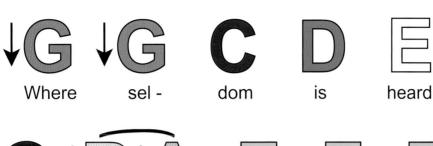

↓G ↓G C D E
Where sel - dom is heard

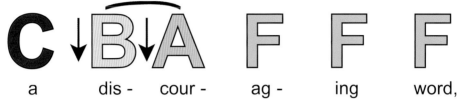

C ↓B A F F F
a dis - cour - ag - ing word,

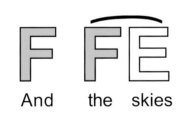

F F E
And the skies

D C ↓B C D C
are not cloud - y all day.

Exploration Fun!

Different ways to use this book...

Gigi ran across the field

Sing the song as you play, or sing the letter names as you play. Which is easier?

Take away the Keyboard Chart and play looking only at the music page, or **close the book** and play by memory. **Close your eyes** and play a song!

Relax your shoulders and arms as you play. **Curve your fingers** a little so that your *fingertips* press the keys. Make up your own finger exercise warm-ups.

Use your LEFT hand thumb to play every **C** in a song, or choose your own fingering for a song. Is the song easier to play?

Find a different group of two black keys and put the dog in that doghouse. Play your song there. Is it high or low? Do you like how it sounds?

Make up a song! ➡

Make Up a Song...

Get a sheet of paper and draw a picture for your song at the top like this.

➡️

Write your song's name under the picture like this. ~~Alive~~ ~~MMM~~ Alive

Write how to play your song:

~~allegro~~ Slow _____   low _____   Kylee ❤️

    fast or slow?   high or low?   Write your name here.

> Write the letters of your song here.   Use any letters you like.
> Make a **pattern** with some of the letters.   Play your song!

G C E G   A D

_____

B E E   A G

_____

B E A   G E

_____

C D E   E G

_____

59

If You're Happy and You Know It

Allegro (ah-leh-groh) - this song is *lively and quick.*

Singing Game

↓**G**
If

↓**GC**
you're hap -

CC
py   and

CC
you   know

C↓B
it   clap

CD
your hands,

(clap, clap)

↓**G**
If

↓**GD**
you're hap -

DD
py   and

DD
you   know

DC
it   clap

DE
your   hands,

(clap, clap)

60

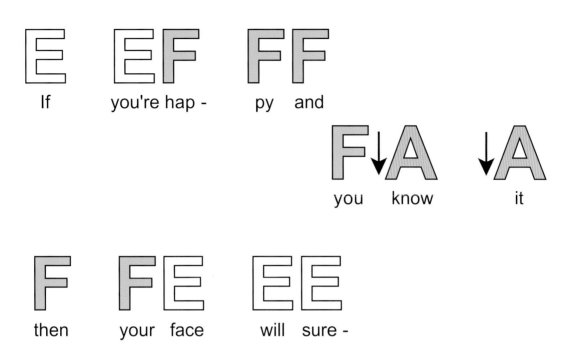

E   EF   FF
If   you're hap -   py and

F↓A ↓A
you know   it

F   FE   EE
then your face will sure -

DC C
ly show   it,

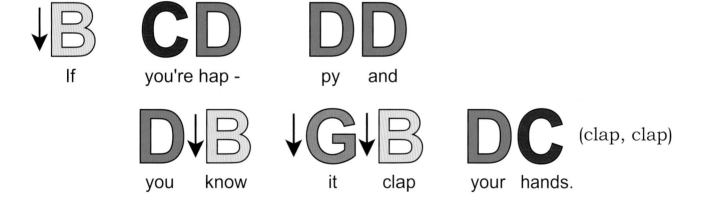

↓B CD DD
If you're hap - py and

D↓B ↓G↓B DC   (clap, clap)
you know   it clap your hands.

Verses:
   change "clap your hands" to

- stamp your feet (stamp, stamp)
- slap your sides   (slap, slap)
- shout Hooray!   (Hoo-ray!)

61

Teddy Bear Song

Spiritoso (spiri-toh-soh) - *lively*.

Rope Jumping Song

F F D
Ted - dy bear,

F F D
Ted - dy bear,

F G F D
Turn a - round —,

F **F** **D**
Ted - dy bear,

F **F** **D**
Ted - dy bear,

D **C** ↓**B**♭
Touch the ground.

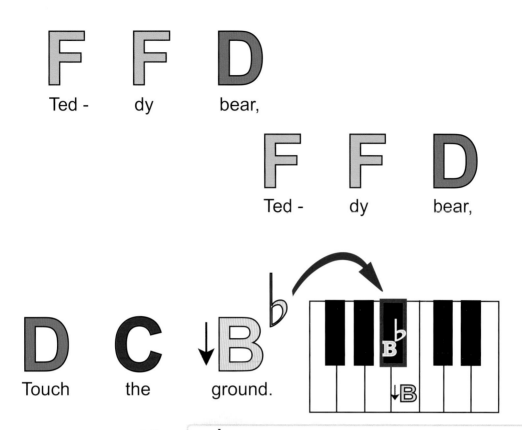

♭ - this *flat sign* tells you that the 𝔹 you play is **flat** - it's the black key on the left side of ↓𝔹.

Verses:

Teddy bear, Teddy bear,
Show your shoe,
Teddy bear, Teddy bear,
That will do.

Teddy bear, Teddy bear,
Go upstairs,
Teddy bear, Teddy bear,
Say your prayers.

Teddy bear, Teddy bear,
Switch off the light,
Teddy bear, Teddy bear,
Say good night.

Westminster Chimes

Largo (lahr-goh) - play *very slowly*.

Played by the bells of the British Houses of Parliament

Ding,   dong,   dong,   ding!

⌐‾‾‾‾‾‾¬ - damper pedal sign: *press and hold the foot pedal down to make ringing bell tones**.

Hear   the   bells   ring!

E From **D** the **C** high ↓**G** tower,

↓**G** Now **D** hear **E** the **C** hour!

↓**F** One! ↓**F** Two! ↓**F** Three! ↓**F** Four!

*Some pianos have two or three pedals. The *damper pedal* is the foot pedal on the right side.

The Eensy Weensy Spider

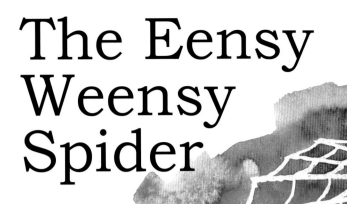

Allegretto (ah-leh-gret-oh) -
lively and quick, but not too fast.

Finger Play Game

↓**GC** **CC** **DE** E

The een – sy ween – sy spi – der

ED **CD** **EC**

went up the wa – ter spout.

E E **FG** G

Down came the rain and

F **EF** **GE**

washed the spi – der out.

66

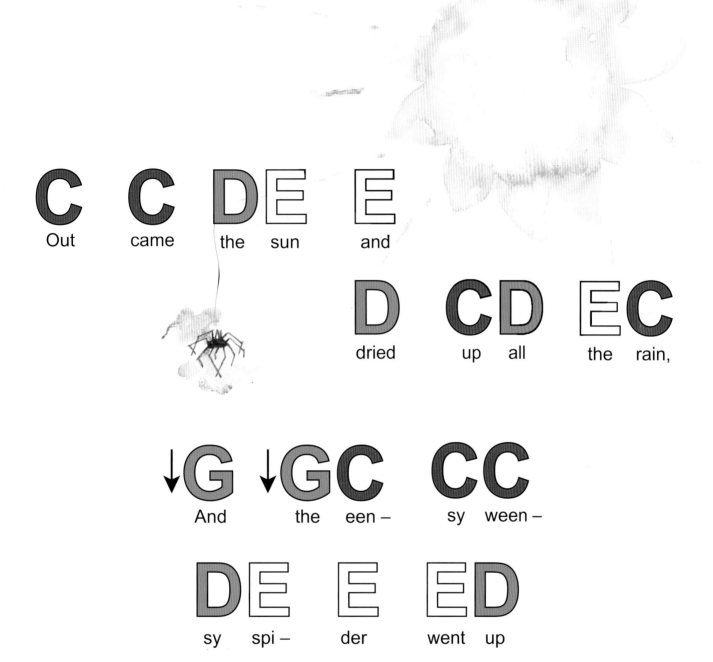

C C D E E
Out came the sun and

D CD EC
dried up all the rain,

↓G ↓GC CC
And the een – sy ween –

DE E ED
sy spi – der went up

CD EC
the spout a - gain.

She'll Be Comin' Round the Mountain

Railroad Song - 1890's

↓G ↓A C C C C C ↓A ↓G

She'll   be   com -   in'   round   the   moun -   tain

> ↓E is one key below
> ↓F. Play it with your
> **LEFT hand pinky** ⑤.

↓E ↓G C

when   she   comes, —

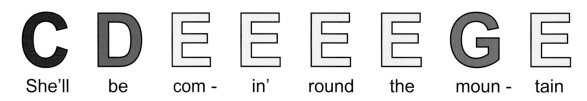

C D E E E E E G E

She'll   be   com -   in'   round   the   moun -   tain

D C D

when   she   comes, —

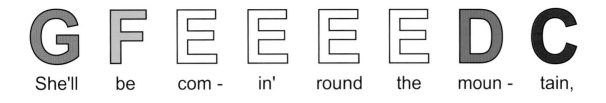

G F E E E E D C
She'll be com - in' round the moun - tain,

C C A A A A D C
She'll be com - in' round the moun - tain,

B A G G C D E D
She'll be com - in' round the moun - tain

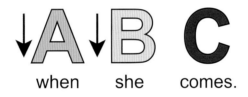

A B C
when she comes.

Verses:

2. She'll be driving six white horses when she comes,
   She'll be driving six white horses when she comes...

3. Oh, we'll all go out to meet her when she comes,
   Oh, we'll all go out to meet her when she comes...

4. And we'll all have chicken and dumplings when she comes,
   And we'll all have chicken and dumplings when she comes...

5. She'll be wearing red pajamas when she comes,
   She'll be wearing red pajamas when she comes...

Oh, Susanna

Allegro (ah-leh-groh) - *lively, quick.*

Stephen Foster

Oh,   I   come

from

Al —

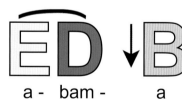

a - bam - a

with

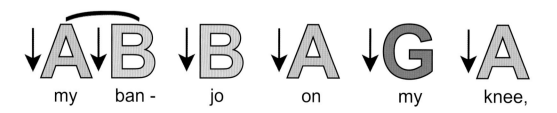

my   ban -   jo   on   my   knee,

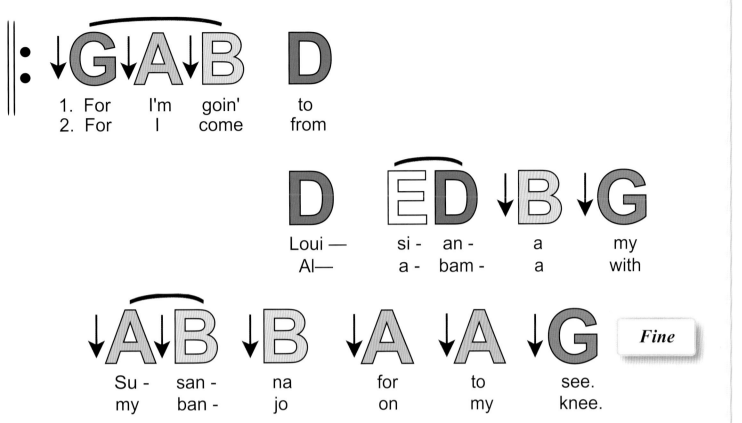

Fine

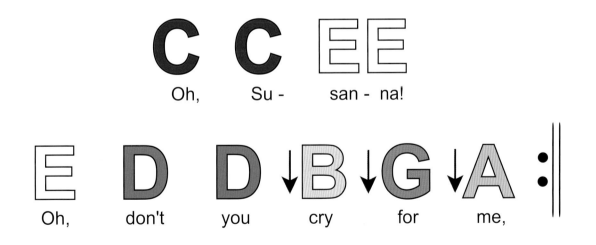

‖: :‖ - *repeat signs:* play this page from the top again with the second verse. Stop at *Fine* (fee-nay) which means *The End*.

Three Blind Mice

Vivace (vee-vah-chay) - *very lively and quick.*

Old Round

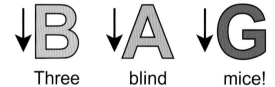

Three	blind	mice!

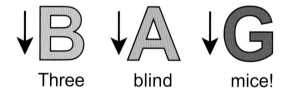

Three	blind	mice!

Play **D** with your **right hand thumb**.
Play **C** with your **left hand thumb**.

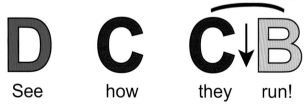

See	how	they	run!

See	how	they	run!

♯ - this *sharp sign* tells you that the F you play is **sharp** - it's the black key on the right side of F.

D G   G
They   all   ran

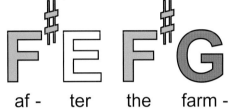

F♯ E   F♯ G   D D
af - ter   the   farm -   er's   wife,

D G G G
She   cut   off   their

F♯ E   F♯ G   D D
tails   with   a   carv —   ing   knife,

D D D G   G
Did   you   ev —   er

F♯ E   F♯ G D D D
see   such   a   sight   in   your   life,

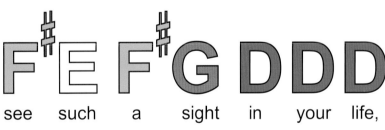

C ↓B   ↓A   ↓G
as   three   blind   mice?

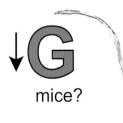

73

The Bear Went Over the Mountain

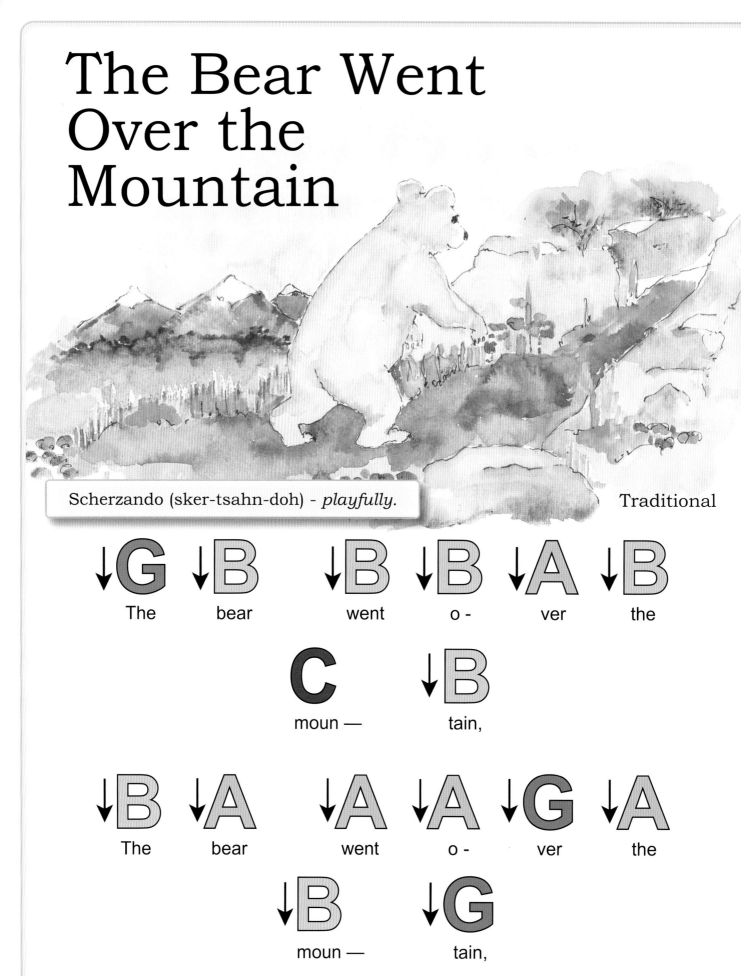

Scherzando (sker-tsahn-doh) - *playfully.*

Traditional

↓**G** ↓**B** ↓**B** ↓**B** ↓**A** ↓**B**

The   bear   went   o -   ver   the

C ↓**B**

moun —   tain,

↓**B** ↓**A** ↓**A** ↓**A** ↓**G** ↓**A**

The   bear   went   o -   ver   the

↓**B** ↓**G**

moun —   tain,

↓G ↓B ↓B ↓B ↓A ↓B
The bear went o - ver the

C Ȇ
moun — tain,

⌢• - this is a *fermata* (fehr-maht-ah) - hold this 𝔼 extra long.

E D
to see

D C
what he

↓A ↓G
could see.

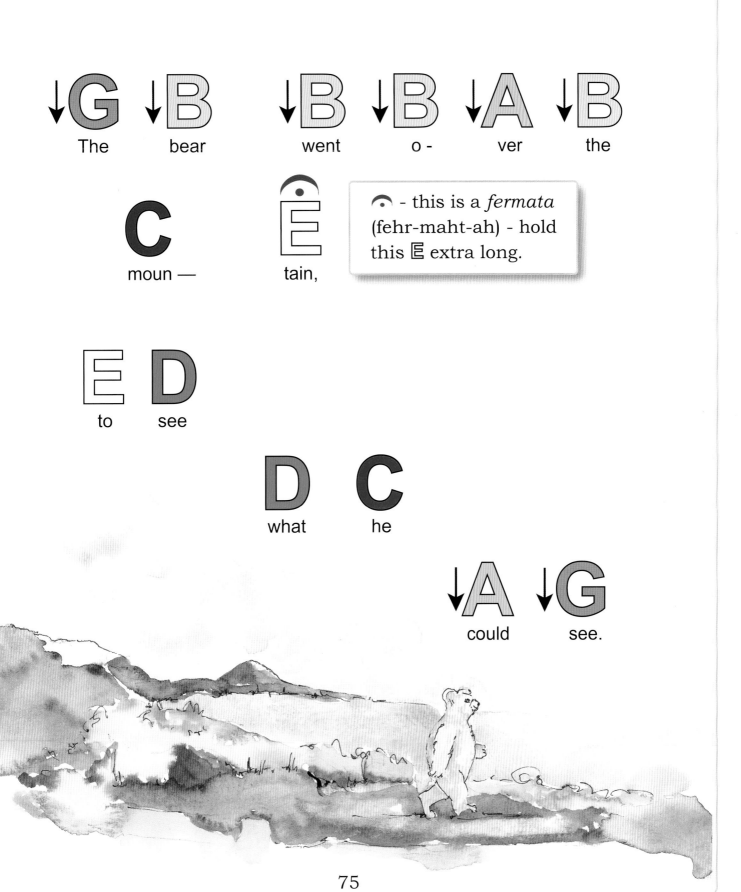

75

America

Maestoso (mah-ess-toh-soh) -
play with *majesty and dignity.*

Words by Samuel Francis Clark
Music by Henry Carey

My   coun -   try   'tis   of   thee,

Sweet   land   of   lib —   er -   ty,

Of   thee   I   sing;

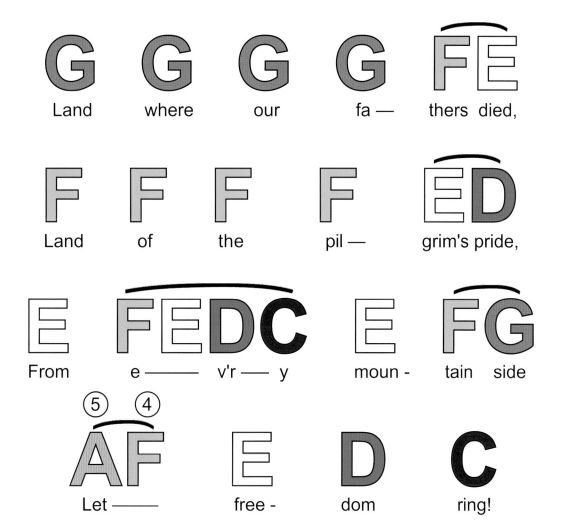

Verses:

2. My native country, thee,
   Land of the noble free,
   Thy name I love.
   I love thy rocks and rills,
   Thy woods and templed hills,
   My heart with rapture thrills
   Like that above.

3. Let music swell the breeze,
   And ring from all the trees
   Sweet Freedom's song.
   Let mortal tongues awake,
   Let all that breathe partake,
   Let rocks their silence break,
   The sound prolong.

4. Our fathers' God, to thee,
   Author of liberty,
   To Thee we sing.
   Long may our land be bright
   With Freedom's holy light,
   Protect us by Thy might,
   Great God, our King.

Glossary

**Look for these italian words at the beginning of some songs.
They tell you how to play a song.**

Allegretto: (ah-leh-gret-oh)....................lively, quick, a little slower
than allegro

Allegro: (ah-leh-groh)............................lively, fast, cheerful

Dolce: (dol-chay).....................................sweet, gentle, soft

Giocoso: (joh-koh-soh)...........................merry, happy

Grave: (grah-veh)....................................slow, solemn

Largo: (lahr-goh).....................................very slow, stately

Leggiero: (leh-djer-oh)...........................light, delicate

Maestoso: (mah-ess-toh-soh)..............with majesty and dignity

March..music for a parade

Scherzando: (sker-tsahn-doh)..............playful

Spiritoso: (spiri-toh-soh)......................lively, with spirit

Soave: (swa-vay)....................................smooth, gentle

Vivace: (vee-vah-chay)...........................very lively and quick

Other words and signs used in this book:

Chorus: (kor-us)......................................repeated part of a song

Damper pedal sign............⌞__⌟............press and hold the foot
pedal down (*see pg. 65)

D.C.al Fine...............**Da Capo al Fine**.....play from the beginning
to **Fine** (the end)

Fermata: (fehr-maht-ah)....⌢.............hold key extra long

Fine: (fee-nay)....................**Fine**...............the end of a song

Flat..♭..............play the very next key to
the left - black or white

Forte: (for-tay).....................f.................play loudly

Piano: (pyahn-oh)...............p..............play softly

Repeat signs....................‖: :‖..........play the part between these
signs again

Round...a song for several voices, each
voice starting a little later

Sharp..♯..............play the very next key to
the right - black or white

Verse..different words for part
of a song

Index of Song Titles

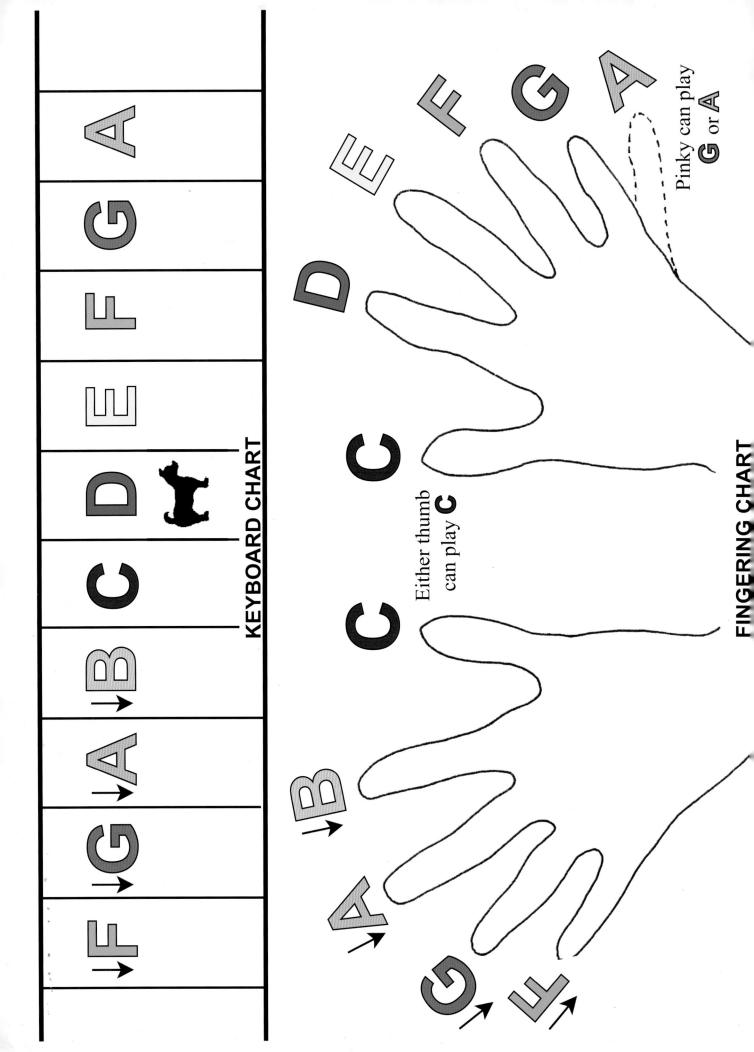

KEYBOARD CHART

FINGERING CHART

Either thumb
can play **C**

Pinky can play
G or **A**